The Unconscious

by

Robert C. Murphy, M.D.

Pendle Hill Pamphlet 325

About the Author

Robert Murphy and Georgia Foster, his wife, live and work in the high mountain county of Wyoming. He is a physician/psychiatrist; she, a specialist in learning disabilities, with the schools.

Singly or together, they are involved in issues of human rights, the environment, homelessness (yes—even in Wyoming), death penalty, violence to women, and Quaker concerns. They also find Wyoming to be a congenial and satisfying home state.

Bob's first Pendle Hill pamphlet, *Psychotherapy Based on Human Longing,* was published in 1960. Because thirty-five years ago *longing* had not been widely recognized as a basic human drive, the pamphlet met an unarticulated need in psychotherapists and psychiatrists countrywide.

Since that time psychotherapy, largely in the hands of non-medical practitioners, has become strongly based on human longing, while more orthodox psychiatry, with its explosion of new research findings in neurobiology, has drifted away from its earlier reliance on the creative Unconscious. Much of psychotherapy has become focused on mind and spirit, psychiatry on brain and pharmacology.

This paper attempts to make the genius of the Unconscious fascinating to readers.

ISBN 0-87574-325-0

Library of Congress catalog card number 96-67671

February 1996: 2,500

A Story

On October 13, 1994 we drove to the airport in Billings, Montana, in order to fly East the following morning for a visit with my children and grandchildren. That morning I packed, finished all current business, loaded the car, and picked up Georgia from her work place. She was to put me on the plane the next morning and then drive back home.

When we checked into the motel at Billings, I said I wanted to put some things into my suitcase before it was finally closed for the trip. As I turned from our room back toward the car I was seized by a horrible emptiness in my belly. I tried to brush it off, but the moment I opened the trunk I saw that it was true; I had left my fully packed suitcase on the floor of our living room.

I went into shock. We left the motel and went to keep a supper date with Billings friends. They were kind and sympathetic, but I could hardly speak. Soon, we were driving back home, intending to return to Billings that same night.

It was my bewilderment at such unprecedented behavior that threw me. You don't do something like that by accident; what does it *mean?* Georgia listened to my struggles for understanding. At about midpoint in our drive home we realized that the return trip to Billings in the same night would be more than we could manage. We decided to postpone my flight twenty-four hours, in the hope that I could get the same one a day later.

Soon after that decision I said: "I could have used these twelve days for finishing the manuscript [of a book I had nearly completed] instead of going East. With my patients canceled and no one knowing I'm in town, I could have it done in that time." A few minutes later Georgia asked: "Did anything happen to that knot in your stomach when you said that?"—and to my surprise I realized Yes, that the knot I had spoken of had eased just as I said those words.

The meaning of the "mistake" then began to—and over the next twenty miles did—become clear: I am to cancel the long-awaited trip and not go East at all, now. We got home at midnight, and I called my daughter, Jennifer (two a.m. her time). She and her housemates had planned a special celebration for my arrival. When I told her what had happened she laughed, said they would miss me a lot, and added: "Would you remember last summer when your daughter canceled a trip to you at the last minute because she had to paint?" I began to feel easier.

As it turned out, that time was not perfect for my trip, anyway. I had sort of grabbed it to use before the expiration of a free flight ticket I had been holding.

The ticket expired, and I did—gratefully—finish writing my manuscript.

Note the precision with which the correction of my trip was designed. Had I remembered my luggage halfway to Billings we would have turned around, driven the additional 130 miles, and loaded ourselves late that night into the motel so that I could fly on schedule the next morning. But no, my inner guide arranged the discovery where it would pack its greatest possible wallop; it wasn't until we were in the motel room that I experienced—as a sudden visceral emptiness—the missing suitcase. The message was: Now it's too late; you've *got* to make some other plan.

That is highly characteristic of unconscious functioning; to keep right on target and to take into account the minutest of details. I had been regretting losing the twelve days on my manuscript, but had told myself that I'll make it up when I get back. My unconscious said "No—this *is* your time for writing; your children and grandchildren can wait—and furthermore, they will understand."

Introduction to the Unconscious

You will recognize in the above story my trust of the unconscious. It does more than make carefully designed corrections in our plans. It has been the source of all that is most satisfying in our lives since long before the word "unconscious" was coined. Before Freud or Jung or Wilhelm Reich or the American Psychoanalytic Association, there were the *atman* of Vedantic philosophy and "The Cloud of Unknowing" of Christian mysticism and the Vision Quests of the first Americans. For millennia seekers have been recognizing the unconscious as the wellspring of spiritual knowing, and devising ways to bring it to consciousness. The unconscious in its deepest and least accessible reaches is our spiritual connection to the Universe. Zen students, Christian and Jewish mystics and countless unknown monastics have devoted their lives to bringing that connection into conscious awareness.

Religious groups exist everywhere that recognize our direct relationship to the divine—the "Inner Light" or "Seed of God," of Quakers. This relationship is, for the most part, unconscious, and can in most circumstances be brought to partial consciousness only through long and disciplined work. Study of the meaning of the unconscious can surely be of value to spiritual seekers, as well as to those whose interest is more secularly in the mind.

In the late 1940s young psychiatrists who had also chosen to become candidates for training in psychoanalysis were given exceedingly heavy doses of Freud. Some of the brightest among us were venturing further, even to speculating on how Werner Heisenberg's "uncertainty principle" in quantum mechanics could help in our understanding of human psychological and behavioral freedom. But I, like most, was a docile and obedient candidate eager to please my teachers; I struggled to understand the unconscious in terms of Freud's unyielding determinism—and that was that. It was not until much later that I became acquainted with the modifications and additions to unconscious theory made by Reich, Horney and others, and especially Carl Jung.

In my early eighties I am not sure what contribution each of those theorists has made to my grasp of the human unconscious. I do know something of that vast psychological/spiritual region in myself, also in my patients, and as it is revealed in poetry and in perceptive fiction—and in spiritual seeking in all of us. The following synthesis denies nothing of what I have learned, but it is mine.

Most of our awareness of the unconscious comes not in dramatic upheavals like my "mistake," but at the interface between conscious and unconscious. That is where you are when you can't remember someone's name, and a few moments later do. The interface is a daily experience for most of us. But mental processes which keep their own schedule about when and if they are ever to be known, are easily brushed aside. Furthermore, it is scary to acknowledge that we don't control all of our psychological processes.

Belief in the unconscious takes courage. That courage can be gained through our understanding that all creativity begins there. Our experience of being not necessarily *immortal,* but in a sense *indestructible*, arises from the unconscious. The unconscious is like an anchor holding us fast to the entire Universe. Recognizing that connection, we experience the same limitlessness that we sense in the Universe itself. When we cling to conscious-only experience, we see ourselves as isolated, separate from it all. In that position our lives retreat, instead, into a narrow and closeted space.

That fenced-in existence results in a stubborn unwillingness to tolerate ambiguity: "Well," grown-ups said to me when I was little, "If you can't explain it then it can't be very important." The conscious-only person is a standard caricature driving people crazy in sitcoms; Archie Bunker in *All in the Family* was often a wonderfully funny example. Our laughter at him recognizes the creativity that is so grotesquely missing from his awareness. Alfred North Whitehead used to describe such characters as: "the clear headed man," meaning the person who values absolute clarity at the expense of the ocean of mentation that underlies and supports it.

Conscious-only thinking is a flight from that ocean, as if in fear that we might lose our familiar bearings, and drown. Conscious-only may feel safe from anxiety, but it is boring. We are drawn toward our deeper selves where our creative energy awaits its birth. Although its lack of preciseness can at times be frightening, we long for it. It is where we find meaning in our existence.

The unconscious is a different language from that of consciousness. It is not a "language" at all, in the sense of words, for it has none of its own; any words it uses have been borrowed from consciousness. While it sometimes yields specific memories that have been repressed, it is more likely to present not particular images, but an awareness of the wholeness and relatedness of things. Oversimplifying: the unconscious is our awareness of relationship, and the conscious of words and things. They are equally important; without a sparkling conscious life we lose some of our ability for accuracy and scientific thinking, and much of our sense of personal power.

The unconscious is the source of insight. Insight means seeing connections among things which had been perceived as separate. Insight comes as a gift, and is always astonishing: when we find the split between work and play dissolving, and notice that often our work *is* play, we feel a zephyr of happy discovery. When we find that a frightening associate represents an opportunity to practice dealing with toxic and difficult people, our fear is leavened by a sense of adventure. When a physicist discovers the absence of time-sequence in "causal" subatomic events, a fresh understanding of *time* opens up as a whole new world for him/her. These connections are made in the unconscious; the surprise and delight with which they emerge express the hiddenness of their source.

The unconscious is rich, rich in paradox and ambiguity—which are the wellsprings of creativity. It floats above the clouds, and streams beneath the ground making connections, drawing all of life together and making sense out of what it can not by itself sense. It joins with our conscious awareness to become our source of truth. It is not unconscious *memories* that we need, so much as a generosity toward our lives, an asking, a trust. In that sense our attitude toward it may be much like prayer—and perhaps is prayer. As we open our hearts to the unconscious we take part in the peace and passion of life: two faces of the same coin.

The unconscious does store up, and may later release, memories that have been too frightening to recall. Under favorable circumstances (including psychotherapy) later in life they may explode into consciousness. A common one is early sexual abuse which, unless completely repressed, might have prevented a child from growing up with any semblance of sanity. But even explosive recollections in adulthood preserve the goals of the unconscious: connectedness, gentleness, self-forgiveness and spiritual awakening.

The ocean of life that we call the unconscious is the source of our peacefulness and our passion. We become peaceful *because* we are passionate, full of life and enthusiasm. But the leaven of peace can raise the bread of our passions into satisfying loaves only in touch with the air out here where we breathe. Left in the dark of repression our impulses act the way they are regarded: evil. It is in the repression of impulses that we regard as "bad" that we injure ourselves and Earth and each other.

Impulses of anger and rage are good examples. The culture wants to keep our rage in its service, not our own. It picks our enemies for us: Saddam Hussein, for example, in contrast to the spontaneous rage we may feel about our fat military budget and the lack of funding for our infrastructure, our homeless, the environment, child nutrition, and education. The repression of our spontaneous rage and other passions begins early in our childhoods; No, beyond its necessary uses, is a much more common general communication to children than Yes.

But like murder, these emotions will out. Repressed rage drives a child to, or toward: relative helplessness or over ambitious accomplishment, unresponsiveness, unloving-ness—a general picture likely to be at least vaguely disappointing to parents. That our culture routinely pushes American children into some degree of zombie-hood is sometimes vividly demonstrated by our occasional discovery of one who hasn't been thus affected. The difference in sparkle, insight and an easy, unaware self esteem is sometimes exceedingly vivid. But zombie-repressed children have all that sparkle, too, just under the lid. Given a chance, these children recapture their freedom and begin also to sparkle.[1]

The repression of rage has varying, often serious, ill effects on our bodies. Frequently fatal, rage is labeled by some professionals "a killer." Its repression also diminishes the freedom of our spirit, one example being those children whose exuberant explorations have been dulled by our thoughtlessly saying No. Leaders and followers who maintain the status quo are afraid of such passions; these passions promise too much independence. Nearly everyone growing up under the pressure to repress emotion comes to regard her/his own rage as fearful and ungovernable.

But it isn't. Anger is an *impulse* to violence, but when it comes into full consciousness it is likely to be nonviolent. It is a form of energy absolutely essential to our self esteem, and ultimately to our ability to love. When it is repressed it hurts people. An everyday example might be seen in teasing a friend in such a way that our remarks hit her most sensitive spot—then responding to her disguised "ouch!" with: "whatsamatter, can't you take a joke?" In this case energy is squandered in unconsciously—and often elaborately—devising a way to hurt her. Such unconscious designs are carried out with dispatch and with impressive conservation of energy. We don't recognize the violence we fully intend to commit; the impulses are held out of sight and ready to be vehemently denied in case of a confrontation.

The unconscious at all times seeks expression. Under heavy repression, it gains it only indirectly, as in that simple example. The impulse becomes sneaky and violent through being hidden from view. If, on the other hand, one finds a way to speak straight: "I am angry with you," the rage—even when it may have built to fever pitch—can lead to further development of the relationship. It is in this sense that I say the goals of the unconscious are gentleness and self-forgiveness; impulses allowed airing without distortion lead to nonviolent feelings of reciprocity. I do not believe it is possible for an impulse to remain violent when it has been fully explored. Transformation and healing, in one of Freud's more enlightened insights, means: allowing the unconscious to become conscious.

Generally, almost no one believes in the unconscious. Everyone knows it is there, but most of us, most of the time, do not live by it. By living by it, I mean keeping it in the heart: living in trust of what we don't yet know of our thinking and feeling, and inviting it to yield to us its insights. No knowledge is final; there is always truth deeper than our immediate experience. We gain in understanding through a readiness in the back of our minds for it to reveal itself. The more we discover of the unconscious the more fascinated we become by it.

Biofeedback is of interest in this regard. By watching brainwave tracings and other indicators, patients and experimental subjects learn inwardly to open themselves to the peacefulness that dwells in their depths. They "control" their brain waves or skin temperature by deliberately abandoning control of them to the unconscious. High blood pressure, rapid pulse, hyperventilation slide toward normal, and many quieter healing events may take place. This is a fascinating device for bringing people into touch with their unconscious through consciously employed technology.

There is a dynamic opposition between these psychic regions. Consciousness "doesn't want to be bothered" with all that stuff; it wants to accomplish things, and it wants comfort, a painless existence, and as much certainty about its perceptions as it can get. Although we can be grateful for its marvelous inventiveness, our conscious is also the status quo of the mind that would prefer awkward questions not be raised.

Toward that headstrong conscious, the unconscious is like a loving parent. It does not interrupt or insist on being heard; it waits, with courtesy and gentleness, for its deeper experience to be recognized. As people learn to love that underlying ocean of life, they spend their lives attending to it—while carrying out the consciously directed dailiness of their existence. In fact, our daily tasks are accomplished much more efficiently with that sort of openness. When we are functioning with an open gate between conscious and unconscious we have fewer accidents, make fewer mistakes, and attend to our needs more gracefully. We find an unmistakable difference in the functioning of our bodies. You can probably recollect that during times in which you experience yourself "in one piece," your voice becomes mellow and pleasing, typing or playing a musical instrument become accurate and effortless, and you find yourself more graceful and with greater endurance while engaged in sports.

But isn't the unconscious also the source of tremendous violence? Yes, part of the unconscious—the only part that seemed of interest to Freud—is made up of material that has been repressed from consciousness: memories, drives and feelings. It is perhaps the lesser part, but it is very important. As psychic material is banished from consciousness, it sits in the unconscious, watching all the time for a chance to act in some way the conscious won't notice. When it can't find any way, it may build up enough charge to burst out *without* becoming conscious, and take direct charge of behavior. One knows the behavior that is being acted out, but has little understanding of its source or meaning. That may result in suicide, atrocities like the Stockton, California massacre of school children, and thousands of other horrors, extending to the more or less insignificant violences of everyday life: insincerely responding to a friend because you can't find the time it might take to be honest.

Gigantic rage in some of my Vietnam veteran patients was expressed *unconsciously* by torturing prisoners to death with almost no conscious satisfaction or revenge. These were men who had been driven beyond the edge of sanity by finding their lives expendable for a war with neither discernible purpose nor intelligible command. Their rage, having no direct outlet, found its way from unconsciousness to the motor pathways of behavior with almost no conscious awareness of it, and their random torturing, and killing of civilians, became little more than a compensatory power play: "Killing is the greatest trip in the world; it makes you feel like a god." Their rage was overwhelming, but largely as a result of their military indoctrination, remained almost completely out of sight. The motiveless mass murderers whose atrocities are so frighteningly common these days, can be seen as scions of our violent culture who have been given a particularly heavy dose of its ineptness, repression and lack of reliable authority.

Rage, when repressed, is dangerous. When it is brought into full conscious awareness, it can be a powerful force for life, forgiveness and a sense of inner power. Rage—by which I include generically everything from mild annoyance to white heat—is a gift of sheer energy which we can take *inward* as personal, nonviolent power. Certainly there is pain holding it in while refusing the seductive comfort of pretending it really isn't there. But that becomes easier with continuing practice. It is hugely worth it; rage is much too precious to be wasted by merely lashing out at someone. You lose friends doing that. But let a burst of rage-energy fan out through your whole being as a sense of power, and you feel great. When you feel good about yourself you *gain* friends.

Holding it in full consciousness, rage can foster a powerful sense of privacy: My rage is mine; I don't have to share it with anyone until I'm good and ready. No one can get it out of me until I want it out.

Possessing all that energy, even when it is painful, can be enormously empowering. It melts from its locked-up rage compartment into a free form flowing through the whole body—a change *from*: I want to hurt or subdue him, to: I'm not interested in what he thinks; I am in control of my life and can do (and not do) absolutely anything I like. (Furthermore, I may some time find I like the bastard.)

That celebration of freedom represents the same energy that had frozen the whole body in rage. It requires holding rage in full and painful consciousness, while giving up all guarantees that the method will "work." Its transformation is a gift; all we can do is to put ourselves into a position that is most receptive to it.

Having given occasional talks on this subject, I am aware that it may still be difficult to find rage so valuable. I recommend trying it out; there's likely to be no better way to learn what I am talking about.

Our culture is not discriminating in its choice of what to repress; its overall target is passion. Passion—strong feeling, and with it commitment and conviction—leads to individual power. As we come into our innate authority we seek change—and change is the enemy of status quo. The culture, through its deans in industry, medicine, education, politics, religion, the media and—secondarily—parents, is untiringly passing us messages against the danger of too much passion. It leans toward keeping us passive and obedient. By deans, I mean those who profit most from status quo. They pour money and energy, mostly without fully conscious intent, into keeping the status quo unchanged. For fifty-five years I have seen mainstream medicine depriving people of taking their health into their own hands. Some churches so massively offer a pre-digested god that one's own discovery of God becomes blurry, or even no longer possible. Mainstream media have an astonishing ability to champion the status quo, as, for example, representing all of our government's military invasions of third world countries as benign.

The unconscious is quietly on the side of passion and change. It drives toward the self-esteem available from our fully welcomed faculties, especially our sexuality and our spirituality. It seeks also to undermine the culture's repression of anger: rage. For that we may be grateful, for we need our rage, as I have said; it serves our longing for full self possession.

The culture pretends to like sex; short of hiking the wilderness, you can't get for two seconds away from it. But its sexual display is shallow, and repressive against real passion. The culture pretends also to like rage: an executive blows his top, and people express their obsequious admiration: "Now *there's* a man who's gotten over his inhibitions!" But rage that serves self-image like that is not rage, but an act.

Rage, when welcomed, establishes our boundaries. A toddler in the terrible-twos affirms its identity with its terrible "No!"—even at times to an ice cream cone that it may actually want. If needed it adds a tantrum to confirm its selfhood. It teachers me—us—too, who I am and who is not-I. Nothing will do so with more power.

Communing with intimate friends a few years ago, I experienced a sustained explosion of sheer, screaming rage at my long-dead parents. It seemed at the time a final release from the nightmare that my childhood had been, and it greatly helped to free me from their continuing impact on my life. (It also resulted in their becoming more human and acceptable to me.) That was in my mid seventies.

I said that when rage remains unconscious it comes out as violence. But the person unconsciously committing the violence is experiencing not his rage, but a disguised derivative of it. Often it is transformed into a self-righteousness which grants license for all kinds of mischief. Religious moralists don't fee "rage'; they just know—beyond question— what is "right!" But you don't need to be homophobic or xenophobic to indulge in that marvelous sense of power; I think most of us have.

Conscious rage enables us to see: *that* is not I; *this* is where I stop! In the 1960s we heard it in the chant: "Hell no, we won't go!", in the 90s: "I'm queer and I'm here!" Consciousness of our boundaries, although they fluctuate, is what makes possible our condensing and focusing our energy. When we "have no boundaries"—as is sometimes said of persons who seem to flow liquidly all over the place—it becomes impossible to take much of a stand about anything.

*UN*conscious rage is violence. Internationally, it gets presidents and prime ministers explaining with cold logic to the citizenry the need for wars through which hundreds of thousands of men, women and children will eventually die. In everyday life it underlies ordinary insincerity: "Angry with you? Why of course not; I'm *fond* of you; how could I possibly be angry with you?" Violence runs all the way from a teenager with her feet up on the back of the couch one-upping her classmate on the telephone, to government-directed gang rapes and death squads. Such brutality—from my study of random murderers to my experience with spiritually wounded Vietnam veterans—appears usually to be carried out with almost no awareness of angry feeling.

The possession of rage is facilitated through its *non-violent* expression: smashing something, writing poetry passionate enough to carry its force, the screaming rage at my parents that I just described—anything that gets the body in some way involved. Emotions are body-mind phenomena. Except as they have endocrine and muscular components they can not become fully conscious. Even speaking can trigger physiological changes the conscious reflection of which is felt as the emotion. Emotions are impulses to action, and when even substitute action is blocked, so is the feeling. That is, in a nutshell, the great contribution to psychiatry of Wilhelm Reich, who identified muscular armoring as the body's contribution to keeping unwelcome emotions out of consciousness.[2] While most people know that physical rigidity helps maintain rigidity of the personality, Reich studied that phenomenon in minute detail, making it both a theory and muscle-unbinding method of therapy that in well-trained hands can be effective.[3]

The old "James-Lange" theory of emotion, vulgarized as: "You feel afraid *because* you are running from the grizzly bear"—as opposed to running because the bear has frightened you—was an attempt early in this century to express the indivisibility of the human organism. Breathlessly running from the bear expresses the fear, thereby making you more aware that you are frightened. That sounds something like a joke now, but the role of action in bringing the emotion to consciousness is its grain of truth.

Without a partnership with consciousness the unconscious can't deal with chunks of undigested rage, lust, despair, avarice and other emotions. We conscious/unconscious beings need these chunks—out here in the open air, in full awareness. All impulses carry our power. Converting them from inactive, buried, dead chunks of alien feeling into vibrant, living feelings in our full possession, changes us from dragging, half-alive beings into free, creative, imaginative persons able to go where we want to go and to know and do what we want to do. Repression necessarily results in the diminishment of our health. Living free of it, while never completely attainable, is a goal of vibrant good health.

Under repression our creative freedom shrinks to thought and action that can be contained within the boundaries of the status quo, and our behavior is to a significant degree out of our control.

But it is almost impossible to kill all creativity. Quilting, traditionally women's work within the confines of patriarchy, gains a new power in the current explosion of the women's movement and sets out to make some impressive political statements. (My most feminist reader cautions me there is nothing new in women making such statements, and that they always have. But I, for one, am hearing them better, and am moved by them in the political ferment of recent decades.) A few doctors, turning from mainstream medicine's heroic approach to almost everything, make room for themselves and their patients to create a sparkling and humane program for treating coronary disease with yoga and group discussion and laughter—along with the exercise and diet that have already been established. Creative freedom in those doctors freed it in the patients who in turn further inspired the doctors. The 1993 PBS documentary on this project was a joy to watch.

The key to that transformation is to welcome all of our impulses, and to train ourselves to catch those that are barely conscious, before they are lost. Impulses derived from the common phobias can be healed by gradually learning to trust the unconscious. For example, the healing of an impulse to throw ourselves off cliffs or high towers into the open air requires our learning (perhaps through hard and sustained work) that we won't be forced to do so against our will. No matter how "innate" they feel, if we had learned early that we are worthwhile, lovable and esteemed—we would not be afraid that the impulse to throw ourselves off a cliff could take an alien command of our will. So it is with all other impulses. The culture's twin demands about rage are: that we not be angry, and that we learn self-control. Both lay waste our health. To be healthy we *must* be angry about the chains we are invited to accept, and we must give up the notion that control is simply in our own hands. It isn't. Our behavior, in greater or lesser degree, always expresses unconscious needs. "Life is what happens to you while you are making other plans," and plans made without inviting unconscious input are even less secure.

Self-control is bludgeoned into us from birth, and it is little but thought-control. Overtly, "just say no" is advice to teenagers for managing drugs and sex. But it would be naive to miss its real meaning: Don't even *think* about sex! If they (the children) don't *think* about sex then they won't *do* it—is a statement one hundred and eighty degrees opposite to what is actually happening. Even if one can banish most sex-thinking from a youngster's consciousness, that charge of energy condenses in the unconscious like a bomb waiting to explode in sexual or non-sexual behavior almost certain to be destructive.

To the extent we trust our unconscious we have no need to *control* our emotions (although some self-control can fill in for us while we are seeking to develop that trust). Think of how we admire a person who appears completely spontaneous. Spontaneity—sparkling, or quiet and meditative—points to keeping faith with the unfailing reliability of the unconscious. Health means living in graceful harmony with the unconscious. It means opening automatically to it when we don't know what to do. The unconscious is patient, rarely in a hurry, and sees far ahead so that its promptings fit both the immediate and the long term situation. Its management of my aborted trip East exemplifies its exquisite attention to detail.

Living in that kind of trust, we will find that ordinary life emergencies are competently managed by the unconscious. Before we know what to do it is actively in the driver's seat. We learn from those events that we don't have to take control; it will be done for us. Later we may say: I don't know how it happened, but I said [did] exactly the right thing!

I shattered a lip in a fall during a shore-break of a river trip. Back on the water, and not yet fully aware of how badly I was hurt, I announced that I was not going to stop, but would finish the trip as planned. But while I was speaking, my *body* was paddling straight to the opposite bank, where we beached the canoe—soon after which we found help in getting me to emergency care. My unconscious not only knew what must be done, but even recognized the severity of my injury before I could find a mirror to confirm it for myself. A little reflection will turn up countless examples of the unconscious taking command in emergent situations.

You can try that reflection for yourself. Think of some emergency with which you have been faced, and scan it back and forth to see how your unconscious took it over, all or in part. If that doesn't work, then think of your having had to swerve suddenly to avoid something in the road. After being alerted by your conscious, that maneuver was executed entirely by your unconscious—and it is likely, later on, that you couldn't understand how you succeeded in avoiding the disaster. Your passengers, if you had any and if they weren't too shaken up, may have marveled at your "skill," which they mistakenly assumed to be part of your everyday, conscious equipment. (Meanwhile, perhaps you saved the life of an animal, or that of the damfool who pulled out in front of you, or your own.)

Freedom from Repression

Those of us who have suffered height phobias are not likely to climb a tower, lean out, and say "OK, I'm not afraid." Nor are we likely to abandon self-control in other ways before we have had time to build surer safeguards. Teaching children to control their impulses is inferior to, and may not even be compatible with, helping them develop a deep sense of self trust. But to provide them with such learning we adult products of a lame and ailing culture will remake ourselves only through long and steady practice. That means we will have to put up with some self-control while we are learning—and helping our children learn—how to live.

But that context brings back to us the *goal* of living free of repression. There are no impulses that must be repressed, because there are no bad impulses.

I hope that statement astonishes you. It does me, when I give it time to sink in. It represents the demise of externally imposed moralism. Nothing that goes on inside our heads needs to be punished or condemned or controlled. We may not be free to entertain those most frightening to us. But it's OK gradually to learn to. Weird fantasies of violence, inventively deviant sexual impulses, these are some of the "crazy" thoughts to be found behind the civilized facade of many of us. They sometimes make people wonder about their sanity, but they are not crazy. These impulses are foreign bodies pushing, in their unrecognizable costumes, toward consciousness where they can offer us their energy. Keeping them under wraps robs us of energy that might otherwise go into enjoying our lives. When we wholeheartedly welcome these bizarre strangers we become freer and stronger, and we *don't* have to understand what they are all about. We become able to make household pets of them when we find they are, after all, perfectly harmless.

If those of my Vietnam veteran patients who had used farmers plowing their rice paddies for target practice, had enjoyed an opportunity to welcome and *possess* their impulses, their rage might not have burst through to take such catastrophic and *unconscious* charge of their behavior.

School youngsters, falling under the culture's repression of sex, often distort their sexual drives into quasi-sexual boosts to their egos—with the resulting epidemic of pregnancies attendant on what often appears as almost lustless sex.

They are given an immensely confusing double message: "Don't do sex except as morally prescribed," and "Do sex every time you get the chance." Both messages are based on the same repressive cultural canon: sex is under all circumstances to be separated from the rest of life. This cuts them off from their sexuality. It results in devastating repression of sexual feeling combined with what often appears to be passionless promiscuity. If we want our teenagers in good control, the first thing we must hope for is that they experience themselves as fully, and joyfully, sexual. They may still sleep around some, but without inflicting the terrible pain of their cruelties on each other, and without continuing their absolutely catastrophic pregnancy epidemic.

Adolescents in this culture do need an ego boost because by and large they experience themselves overwhelmingly as unloved. That children, and particularly adolescents, are not valued for themselves is illustrated by the way they are enthusiastically consigned *out* of our lives and into serving only as "our future." Adolescents have little recourse except to strike out with their blended peer wisdom, in a groping effort to shape their lives. Adolescence is the hardest time for grown-ups to maintain loving control of their youngsters. Already handicapped by cultural suppression of their personal wisdom, parents may find the cultural and hormonal thrusts that drive their children halfway out of their enfoldment more than they can gracefully handle. Obedient to culturally mandated "expertism," they seem to drift toward consciousness-only functioning, and are robbed of passion and power in nurturing their children. Under massive repression teenagers precariously raise each other.[4]

The unconscious has a thousand ways to make itself known. It is in dreams that we find some of its most creative communications. Night after night it builds complex and wonderfully symbolic dramas, calling to us: "Come! Let's go to the theater." Our dreams, when we remember them, are a source of endless entertainment and instruction. Sometimes dreams are scary. Then they give us a chance to look sidewise into fears otherwise kept out of awareness. Dreams sometimes become the very linchpin of life change; we wake up, and maybe after reflecting on the drama we have just left behind, suddenly find it pulling everything together.

Dreams also fine tune decisions. In symbolic form they may provide us with practice and rehearsal of behavior about which we are unsure in daily life. At other times they give us much needed warnings, designing careful parables in dream-action from which, on awakening, we find new portents. There seems to be no limit to the ways the unconscious finds to guide and order our lives.

Often enough dreams are sheer pleasure. Where else do we find ourselves able to dive off a five-hundred foot cliff, or abandon ourselves without responsibility or guilt to some voluptuous sexual adventure?

And they can be scary as hell—offering us the golden opportunity of recognizing our terror, living through it, and forgiving it.

If dogs dream only about chasing rabbits—although I doubt anyone will ever know—humans dream all of Shakespeare and Great Books and then some. But I don't believe the neofreudian claim that all dreams contain distinct messages; I think most of them remain forever obscure. They may be richly satisfying anyway, and there is a reason for that: they move material from deeper in the unconscious to its more accessible levels, i.e. closer to consciousness.

That can be understood by the common experience in waking life of feeling good (or bad) and then only later realizing it was because of something that you hadn't noticed: being smiled at, half-noticing a lovely flower arrangement, unconsciously making a graceful movement. On such occasions the stimulus for feeling good remained unconscious, but still affected your mood. In the same manner, dreams may do a great deal for us without making us aware of what they are saying. They bring unconscious material closer to consciousness, and leave us feeling generally more in control. If the material—still unconscious—is about a complex of fear and loneliness symbolized by A, then next time we encounter something related to A in waking life we are likely to manage it more creatively.

Analyzing dreams can make them not less, but more, obscure. When we accept their gifts in an intuitive, *dreamlike* way we are speaking their language. People can be made to feel guilty about not "understanding" their dreams. But trying to force dream-meanings into a psychoanalytic or cocktail party setting is a good way to lose them in a deep and prolix fog.

Dreams, understood or not, are gifts; even the terrifying nightmares of my Vietnam combat veterans offer help for their facing agony that still remains to be worked through. I have seen these men become visibly stronger and freer and more resilient when they are held and supported through them.

The same is true of waking impulses that don't feel at all like harmless household pets, but that seem just plain *wrong*. We don't really escape an impulse toward some sexual behavior that could not possibly be integrated into the rest of our life by finding ways to re-banish it from awareness. It is not there by accident, and in some way it is valuable. Furthermore, it may be enjoyable, and *enjoyment*—reflecting a successful lifting of repression—is likely to make it less (not more) dangerous. As we learn to trust our impulses our unconscious will take care of our behavior. But it is not likely to demand that we consciously entertain an impulse too powerful or dangerous for us to handle. No; it knows both our limits and our potentials better than we consciously do, and seeks to protect us from being pushed beyond our tolerance.

Does that mean the unconscious never makes mistakes? Mistakes are made by the unconscious/conscious system acting in isolation. Relying on our depths is an enormous safeguard. But just saying God-be-with-me may not be enough to resolve an issue in human relationships . We also need friends with whom we can explore it. Although the unconscious is reliably-reliable, it is also allied to our fallible egos. For that reason our beliefs and behavior need constant shaping through sharing back and forth in intimate relationships.

That brings us to the no-touch, be-all-you-can-be, independent rugged individualism through which our culture assigns us the most lonely isolation it can get us to accept. Intimacy is dangerous to the status quo; as people share freely together they no longer remain passive and obedient. We are constrained to live in, and find ways to cope with, an isolated, non-intimate society.

But as with quilting, we all have a start on building our freedom. There is no end to exploring intimate contacts. A few words to friends, spouse, or in the safety of communing with a stranger on the plane whom you will probably never see again, all offer themselves for practice in sharing, and in the shaping we all need of our lives.

In that process, the unconscious continues as our guide. If the stranger on the plane gives a subtle sexual response when we are interested in a different form of sharing, we will sense it and move only cautiously ahead. If we get a pre-formed religious response we will know we are probably not going to be heard. The unconscious, which has no senses, is alert to what our eyes and ears tell it, and draws immediate conclusions that are likely to be accurate. We can easily see its power in children, who are famous for spotting negative responses in grown-ups even when they don't know that their own bodies are clearly betraying their distrust. (The same is often true also of animals.)

In tennis and volleyball our behavior is instantly put together by the computer on which we have to rely for most of what we do. Imagine relying on that same computer for decisions about money and sex and other major life choices as easily as you do about hitting a ball with a racket. When we can abandon our lives to our unconscious, we will discover the almost unimaginable freedom in which we have been created.

Living close to the unconscious we are close, also, to the Spirit of the Universe, for at our deepest reaches that is where they meet. The kingdom-of-heaven—on those rare occasions in which it dawns on us that that's really where we are—is a life of power and contentment, even during those times in which we are facing one or another of life's terrible agonies. God rests everywhere, including at the juncture between our unconscious and the Infinite.

We don't need to be too concerned about what is "right" because the inner guide already knows. Goals like trying to "be more forgiving" can violate our integrity. Those qualities are already seeded for us in the unconscious. There is a difference between living in trust of our depths and what is sometimes meant by trying to "do God's will." The latter may be weighted with moralisms: "beliefs" that we have to live up to. She/he who visits our deepest selves already *is* love and truth and beauty, honesty, nurture, caring and responsibility. So are we, to the extent we live in that context. Everything is in its place; everything "makes sense"—even though all around us is a world of accelerating violence and environmental decay. Heaven is here, and within us—if we glimpse it once we will remember, and trust and wait. Keeping tuned to our inwardness, we develop habits of behavior which are canons enough.

Ecstasy in the presence of the Spirit may on rare occasions be all consuming: one may be lost in and overwhelmed by the Oneness of all existence. (Such experiences are most common with children—although usually later wiped out of memory under the pressures of status quo living.) In everyday life we experience echoes of that Oneness. They make life enjoyable, generous and loving—and they guide our behavior. They make the standard by which the rest of our experience is measured. The words "I love you"—pleasing under any circumstances—will when one senses in them echoes of the Spirit, be wonderful: full of wonder. A wildflower poking through melting spring snow may for a moment open heaven to one who receives it.

No matter how we practice trusting our depths, we are going to get into situations in which we are too frightened or too angry to be aware of our inner guide. And all too often we just drift out of touch with it anyway. Those are good times to learn to not-do: to say as little and do as little as circumstances will allow. Losing touch is no disaster; the unconscious is pressing toward consciousness. Waiting, our contact with it will return.

The Unconscious and the Body's Health

The unconscious manages the functioning of our bodies and is, of course, in closer touch with our permanently unconscious life-supporting neuroendocrine systems than consciousness could ever be. This connection has been recognized in general medicine roughly since Walter Cannon published *The Wisdom of the Body* earlier in this century.[5] His book popularized words like *adrenaline* and phrases like "fight or flight," and they have been common household intelligence ever since. Physicians have been enchanted by its simple elegance.

But after those early days of sunny innocence come medical technology and the fashions of organized medicine—and we forget. That lovely wonder and excitement go out of the window, and we are back again to the body as machine parts, and to compulsive and fragmenting diagnosis.

Trying to heal the body without reference to the unconscious *as its major source of healing* is absurd. But physicians have largely been trained away from understanding patients as persons. Encountering the near-miracles of healing which are common during medically managed illnesses, they too often brush them off with a word from medicalese: "a spontaneous [or idiomatic] recovery." The unexplained resolutions of cancer, the way people go from death bed to full healing in response to some life-affirming event, may completely escape their notice.

I am sure every physician knows that hypnosis is an accepted treatment for warts—a *viral* condition[6]—and has access to accounts like those of Bernie Siegel[7] and Norman Cousins,[8] making clear that our moods and our beliefs heal or sicken us depending on which way they point. They know that immunological competence is of cardinal importance in the management of cancer; and reports might be found in their waiting room periodicals about the Simonton approach to cancer, based on psychologically improving that competence.[9] They may witness patients waiting for some person to come before allowing themselves to die, and could thus learn that the unconscious *very* frequently decides when the time is right—or may not yet be right—for us to die.[10]

It is hard not to see the impact of mood and feelings on the outcome of heart disease. As for the gastrointestinal tract: even fifty-five years ago we were taught "The GI tract is the mirror of the emotions." Still, it is hard to escape from how four to eight years of intense training has molded us into technicians and out of healing.

I once sat for a bedside consultation with a hospitalized young man in agonizing pain from an ulcerative and hyperactive bowel. There wasn't much I could do, but after about twenty minutes I said four words that seemed to me to point to the heart of what was going on: "Bob, you may die." Within one second, two at the most—the pain stopped. The gut, which I had been hearing and seeing and even feeling through his abdominal wall, went completely quiet. And he became instantly peaceful. (Unfortunately, I did not have an opportunity to follow up on this event; he died a year later from ulcerative colitis.) I find it easier to feel the aptness of my words than to explain them. I think my words granted his tormented body the immense relief of giving voice to what his unconscious was clearly accepting. In some circumstances we fear death. But the thought of death can be wonderfully peaceful. I think my words gave him permission to die. There was no point in his gut protesting any more, after I had spoken them. We (doctors) are taught death is our enemy, but when we dare to accept it as friend we can come to trust it.

Former Pendle Hill director, Dan Wilson, described an occasion of relief from strangling asthma in response to a peaceful insight. Bernie Siegel speaks of a patient recovering from cancer in response to believing in some treatment of questionable value, then dying when told it was really worthless. How is it possible for physicians not to see that body health and spiritual health can not be separated?[11] From my own experience, and from my acquaintance with other physicians, I know many of us welcome the revolution in medicine that seems clearly to be on its way. I hope we can continue to learn more and more from our most ready and accessible instructors, our patients.

A Free Ride

The unconscious, and God who infuses it like a spring at its deepest reaches, make up the paired One that Quakers call "the inner light." This spark of divinity offers us the experience of being unconditionally loved. Experiencing unconditional love frees us from the conflicts that turn one part of us against another. Freedom from conflict integrates our spirits and bodily functions into a single focus of health.

Freedom from conflict includes a bold acceptance of unavoidable pain. Here, as elsewhere, the unconscious must take the lead, for consciousness left to itself will employ a thousand escapes from pain, and pretend it doesn't exist. To the extent it succeeds in this deception, we live uninteresting lives marked by at least a vague sense of unfulfillment.

In this respect the unconscious is a giant towering over its little brother. It says: Give me life—*all* of it, and it struggles against the addictions of the Small One. It wants not to be tied into immobility and impotence. Where the conscious can offer the distractions of workaholism or frenzied sexual escapes or hyperintellectual superiority or one and a thousand other addictions, the unconscious says "No!—Give me my suffering!" It doesn't want *suffering*; it wants the whole sweep of life that includes it. It wants life's central gift: a freedom of spirit and behavior that stretches beyond human imagining.

Freedom frightens people not used to it; it leaves one with no feeling of boundaries.[12] But it is actually opposite to the boundarilessness of persons I mentioned who seem liquidly to flow all over the place. The boundary supplied by freedom is that of my personal limitations. As a carpenter I am not free to cut diamonds for jewelry, or as a psychiatrist to do reconstructive face surgery. As a person with a height phobia you may not be free to stand on the edge of a cliff, or with a social phobia, to do public speaking. Freedom in the sense I am using it makes our boundaries clear by showing us that our power lies, undiminished, *within* them. We are each, within our limitations, a tool for the perfecting of life. That being so, we are in no way limited by the limits of our personalities. We are part of the Infinite.

That means we have the potential for a free ride through life—almost effortless. We can laugh until our bellies ache, cry when we need to, give away our hearts to anyone who will accept them, give away our money within limits of our need for it, live carelessly and delightedly with whatever life brings us including the pleasure we get from our own accomplishments. And get, in good faith, through the dull times and the depressed times when nothing seems any good. (Yes, and gripe and bitch and complain about them, too—for we don't have to be brave!) In Thomas Kelly's words: "Everything matters; nothing matters;"[13] dying, for example, is not particularly important, but how we die certainly is.[14] Having our self-esteem cut down by a sly dig from a friend doesn't matter—being hurt is unpleasant but in the long run unimportant—but how we absorb that pain and let ourselves be stimulated to new insights by it, is. In the light of our relationship to the Universe we are free to accept everything life brings us either from inside or outside, whether they are welcome gifts or unwelcome pain.

In that mindset we live in context with the Universe and are able to care for it (starting with our beleaguered Earth). To do so is the same as listening to the small voice of our unconscious which, through its connection with God, is available as our guide. When we shape its insights by sharing them with each other we have a project for appropriate living which can't be improved on.

Trusting the unconscious does not mean its divine and ultimate center can fix-you-all-up so you live happily ever after. Healing wounded spirits can take a long time. There is a reason for that: it is that we are made in the image of God. Our aim is to come into that heritage; the central seed of body/spirit health waits to be found: pleasure, contentment, laughter, companionship and adoration. If that were easy it would lose its magic.

It is a task not just for this year or the next, but for life. That is OK. The heart knows nothing about time; it just seeks a sense of home and sureness and belonging and love. "Had we but world enough and time ...," the poet complains. Well, we do. There is *time* for everything, and it does not need to be measured.

Notes

1. Lovely examples can be found in Robert Coles' interviews with children. See *The Call for Stories* (Houghton Mifflin, 1989), for example.
2. Reich, Wilhelm, *Character Analysis*, edited by Vivant R. Carfagro, translated from German (F.S.&G., 1980).
3. Baker, Ellsworth, F., M.D., *Man in the Trap: The Causes of Blocked Sexual Energy* (Avon Books, 1967). See also Mann, W. Edward Hoffman, *Wilhelm Reich: The Man who Dreamed of Tomorrow* (Edward, J.P. Tarcher, Inc., 1980).
4. If there is any "must" reading for parents of adolescent girls, and for the girls themselves, it is Mary Pipher's warm-hearted and powerful description of what this age group is up against: *Reviving Ophelia: Saving the Selves of Adolescent Girls* (Ballantine, 1994).
5. Cannon, Walter B., *The Wisdom of the Body* (New York: W.W. Norton, 1932).

6. Weil, Andrew, M.D., *Health and Healing: Understanding Conventional and Alternative Medicine* (Houghton Mifflin Co., 1983), pp. 199–205.

7. Siegel, Bernie S., *Love, Medicine and Miracles: Lessons Learned About Self-healing from a Surgeon's Experience with Exceptional Patients* (New York: Harper & Row, 1986).

8. Cousins, Norman, *Anatomy of an Illness As Perceived by the Patient* (New York: Bantam, 1984).

9. See, for example, Simonton, Stephanie M. with Robert L. Shook, *The Healing Family: the Simonton Approach for Families Facing Illness* (New York: Bantam, 1984).

10. See *Mental Medicine Update* II. 1, Summer/Fall 1993, The Center for Health Sciences, P.O. Box 176, Los Altos, California 94023. The lead article statistically reviews the deaths and birthdays of close to three million people, showing how people *wait* to die when anticipating celebratory events, and hasten dying when there is not much to look forward to.

11. See Siegel, *Love, Medicine and Miracles;* and Weil, *Health and Healing,* pp. 238ff; and Pelletier, Kenneth, *Holistic Medicine; From Stress to Optimum Health* (Delacorte Press/Seymour Lawrence, 1979), p.113ff; and Capra, Fritjof, *The Turning Point: Science, Society and the Rising Culture* (New York: Bantam, 1982), pp. 352–58.

12. See, for example, Erich Fromm, *Escape From Freedom* (Avon, 1976), especially Chapter 5, pp. 136-206.

13. Kelly, Thomas, *A Testament of Devotion* (Harper-SF, 1941).

14. Four wonderful books on dying: Levine, Stephen, *Who Dies: An Investigation of Conscious Living and Conscious Dying* (Anchor Books, Doubleday, 1982); Easwaren, Eknath, *Dialogue With Death: A Journey Through Consciousness* 2nd ed. (Nilgiri Press, 1992); Kubler Ross, Elisabeth, *Death: the Final Stage of Growth* (Prentice Hall, 1975); and Sherwin B. Noland's balance to any over-romantization of death, in *How We Die* (Knopf, 1994).